THE FISHERMEN SLEEP
DIE FISCHER SCHLAFEN

Sabine Lange
THE FISHERMEN SLEEP
DIE FISCHER SCHLAFEN

൦ൟ

Translated by Jenny Williams
Introduced by Mary O'Donnell

2005

Published by Arc Publications,
Nanholme Mill, Shaw Wood Road
Todmorden OL14 6DA, UK

Copyright © Sabine Lange 2005
Translation copyright © Jenny Williams 2005
Introduction copyright © Mary O'Donnell 2005

Design by Tony Ward
Printed at Antony Rowe Ltd
Eastbourne, East Sussex

ISBN 1 904614 20 5

ACKNOWLEDGMENTS

Immer zu Fuß was published by
Federchen Verlag, Neubrandenberg,
Germany, in 1994

Cover picture 'Boot an Land' by Sabine Curio,
reproduced by kind permission of the artist.

The publishers acknowledge financial assistance
from ACE Yorkshire

Arc Publications: 'Visible Poets' series
Editor: Jean Boase-Beier

CONTENTS

Translator's Preface / 9
Introduction / 15

22 / Windfreund	Windfriend / 23
22 / Die Winter	The Winters / 23
24 / In der erstbesten Etüde von Chopin	In the Next Best Étude by Chopin / 25
26 / Mein Schuh	My Shoe / 27
26 / Terrasse	On the Terrace / 27
28 / Fallada-Archiv	Fallada Archive / 29
28 / Nach einem Regen	After a Shower of Rain / 29
30 / Morgens	In the Morning / 31
30 / Toccata	Toccata / 31
32 / Beginnende Tropfen	The First Drops / 33
34 / Gelassenheit	Composure / 35
36 / Dauerfrost	Permafrost / 37
38 / Ernte 86	Harvest 86 / 39
40 / Vergeblich	In vain / 41
42 / Gedanke	Thought / 43
44 / Am Baum…	Against the tree… / 45
44 / Leben mit der Schneeschippe	Life with the Snow Shovel / 45
46 / Sonntags	On Sundays / 47
46 / Man sagt	They Say / 47
48 / Einfache Bewegung	A Simple Movement / 49
48 / Igelstunden…	Hedgehog seasons… / 49
50 / Bäume	Trees / 51
52 / Abends…	In the evenings… / 53
52 / Fragment	Fragment / 53

54 / Katze	Cat / 55
56 / Zaungast	Eavesdropper / 57
58 / In eine Decke gehüllt	Wrapped up in a Blanket / 59
58 / Wege	Paths / 59
60 / Gruß	A Greeting / 61
60 / Vier Worte	Four Maxims / 61
62 / Bohnenwerder	The Bohnenwerder Island / 63
64 / Im Traum	In my Dreams / 65
64 / Feldberger Abendstille	Evening Stillness in Feldberg / 65
66 / Der Vorsichtige	The Cautious Man / 67
68 / Brot und Wein	Bread and Wine / 69
68 / Zustand	Condition / 69
70 / Fasching	Carnival / 71
70 / Verband	Conjunction / 71
72 / Still-Leben	Still-Life / 73
74 / Müde genug	Tired Enough / 75
76 / Rückspiegel	Rearview Mirror / 77
76 / Aufstieg	Ascent / 77
78 / Und es uns forttreibt ...	And it Drives us on.... / 79
78 / Brunnen	Wishing Wells / 79
80 / Safari	Safari / 81
80 / Doch aus meinem Gesicht	But from my Face / 81
82 / Rückzuck	Jump Start / 83
82 / Störung	Interruption / 83
84 / Apfelspruch	Apple Proverb / 85
84 / Steilufer	Steep Bank / 85

86 / Spaß	Good Times / 87
86 / Gedenkminute	A Minute's Silence / 87
88 / Gesagt	Past and Present / 89
88 / Wenn du eine Liebe hast …	When you Have a Love … / 89
90 / Schneidegras	Cutting Grass / 91
92 / Liebesgedicht	Love Poem / 93
94 / Kaufhaus	Department Store / 95
96 / Berührung	Contact / 97
96 / Briefe	Letters / 97
98 / Kommunikation	Communication / 99
98 / Alle Boote	All the Boats / 99
100 / Schleifende Vögel	Flightless Birds / 101
102 / Körner	Seed / 103
102 / Kindheit	Childhood / 103
104 / Erinnerung	Memory / 105
104 / Reste des Sommers	Remnants of Summer / 105
106 / Haus im Norden	House in the North / 107
106 / Das Meer	The Sea / 107
108 / Terrasse II	On the Terrace II / 109
108 / Regen	Rain / 109
110 / Ich sah dich	I saw You / 111
110 / Kleine Nachtwache	A Little Night Watch / 111
112 / Die Fischer	The Fisherman / 113

Biographical Notes / 115

SERIES EDITOR'S NOTE

There is a prevailing view of translated poetry, especially in England, which maintains that it should read as though it had originally been written in English. The books in the 'Visible Poets' series aim to challenge that view. They assume that the reader of poetry is by definition someone who wants to experience the strange, the unusual, the new, the foreign, someone who delights in the stretching and distortion of language which makes any poetry, translated or not, alive and distinctive. The translators of the poets in this series aim not to hide but to reveal the original, to make it visible and, in so doing, to render visible the translator's task too. The reader is invited not only to experience the unique fusion of the creative talents of poet and translator embodied in the English poems in these collections, but also to speculate on the processes of their creation and so to gain a deeper understanding and enjoyment of both original and translated poems.

Jean Boase-Beier

TRANSLATOR'S PREFACE

Translators find their authors – and authors their translators – in many different ways and translators' motives can range from the mercenary to the messianic. In the case of this anthology, the translator has known the author for some twenty years and when Sabine Lange's first volume of poetry appeared in 1994 I was convinced that it deserved a much wider audience.

This translation has been a collaborative one in the sense that the poet, who speaks very little English, has taken a personal interest in the project. She has been unfailingly helpful and forbearing in responding to my queries. A key point in the development of the translations was our participation in an advanced course in Literary Translation at the University of the Saarland in 1998: here we held workshops with students in Translation Studies which proved extremely stimulating and encouraging.

Sabine Lange's poetry explores the human, and especially the female, condition in the light of her own experience as archivist, musician and poet and is set against the backdrop of the beautiful and unspoilt Mecklenburg countryside in which she has spent most of her life. My friendship with the poet and my familiarity with Mecklenburg were two enormous assets in approaching the task of translation. I am also indebted to the postgraduate students at Dublin City Universtiy who took part in the German Literary Translation module in 2005 for their helpful comments in the final stages of the translation.

It is clearly an advantage to be able to picture the (former) Fallada Archive in Feldberg when dealing with 'Fallada-Archiv' or to have spent some lazy summer afternoons on the 'Bohnenwerder' in Carwitz to understand the magical quality evoked in the poem of the same name. I have attended musical recitals given by the poet and accompanied her to concerts, which has afforded me insights into Lange's relationship to music – although her music poems have a universal appeal. As a woman it is not difficult to sympathize with the sentiments expressed in such love poems as 'Tired Enough' (p. 75), 'A Minute's Silence' (p. 87) and 'Interruption' (p. 83). The poems which explore the self and childhood – 'Fragment' (p. 53), 'Childhood' (p. 103), 'Memory' (p. 105) – are ones with which many readers will be able to identify.

While a profound knowledge of Sabine Lange's life, her interests and concerns are indispensable for anyone who wishes to translate her work, such knowledge in itself is insufficient to produce appropriate translations.

My principal aim as translator was to convey as much of the essence of Lange's poetry as possible in English. It was therefore important for me to retain as much of the rhythm, rhyme and linguistic sophistication as I could – even if that meant sometimes straining English syntax to its limits.

In the case of 'Conjunction' (p. 71) it was relatively easy to convey the playfulness and profundity of the German poem which ponders the significance of the connector 'and' in the phrase 'you and I':

> you and I
> we lived conjoined
> by connectors
> saying nothing and yet
> connecting...

The alliteration in the next poem 'Still-Life (p. 73), which deals with a marriage in difficulties, was equally straightforward to translate:

> and the parents slice
> the salami in silence.

Lange's ability to encapsulate her ideas in deceptively simple language and very short lines provided a much bigger challenge. The last four lines of the eight-line poem

'Man sagt' / 'They Say' (p. 47) is a good example of this:

> doch es ist
> *yet   it is*
> wie im Traum und man träumt
> *as in-a dream and one dreams*
> dass man geht
> *that one   goes/walks*
> und geht kaum.
> *and goes hardly*

While it is possible to retain the same number of syllables in lines 3 and 5, it proved impossible to translate line 6 with 6 syllables and line 8 with 3 syllables in English. An additional difficulty was posed by the extremely common verb 'gehen' (to go): neither 'go', which cannot stand alone in this context, nor 'walk' which is too explicit, are appropriate. In the end 'gehen' was translated by 'move'.

The verb 'gehen' runs as a leitmotif through these poems. The title of the original German collection *Immer zu Fuß* (literally: always on foot) is completed by this verb which in everyday language means to walk as opposed to using any form of propulsion, be it combustion or jet engine or even pedal power. In Lange's work 'to go on foot' denotes a certain relationship with the earth, a rootedness in the natural environment, a decision to live one's life in tune with nature.

As the previous example shows, however, it is not always possible to translate 'gehen' with 'go'. In German most verbs of motion can be based on 'gehen' by adding appropriate prefixes, in English this is often theoretically possible – to go away, to go up, to go down – but considerations of rhythm, metre and poetic style often dictate the use of forms such as 'leave', 'ascend', 'descend' and so on.

When poems with very short lines also have rhymes, as in the seven-line 'Fragment' (p. 53), the task is made all

the more formidable. The last four lines contain the rhyme
'Ganz' / 'Tanz':

> ein Stückl   Bruch
> *a little-piece something-broken*
> von einem Ganz
> *from   a   whole*
> der Meister ging zu früh
> *the master   went too early*
> zum Tanz
> *to-the dance*

Here the poet sees herself as a fragment of a sculpture that was never finished because the sculptor preferred to do something quite frivolous rather than complete the serious work in hand, i.e. the poet. I came up with three possible translations for the 'Ganz' / 'Tanz' rhyme:

> a tiny piece
> of a great whole
> the sculptor left early
>
> to rock 'n' roll

and the alternatives: 'of a grand design ... / to wine and dine'; 'of a work of art ... / to follow his heart'. Finally, the first translation was chosen as it mirrors the German most closely.

The end rhymes in 'Evening Stillness in Feldberg' (p. 65) and 'A Little Night Watch' (p. 111), which both have more or less regular rhythms, could be reproduced in English which has similar poetic forms. However, the rhyme, combined with assonance, at the end of 'A Greeting' (p. 61) presented an interesting case. In this poem the poet contrasts 'the living', i.e. the people involved in the hustle and bustle of life whom she links to the clear blue of the sky and the water, with 'the scribes', i.e. the poets whom she describes as grey: 'stillverdrossen grau / und ungenau'. Here the notion of 'verdrossen' (morose) was abandoned in order to preserve the rhyme and the effect of the assonance: 'silently melancholy / grey and shadowy'. Poetry translation is often a case of establishing priorities; here rhyme and poetic effect took precedence over exact reproduction of meaning.

A striking aspect of Sabine Lange's poetry lies in the images it evokes. These images can often be translated without much difficulty: for example, the image in 'A Simple Movement' (p. 49) of the poet taking her hands out of a bucket of slops and shaking 'the caustic scum off the / back of my hands the spray / of the slobbering mouths' as a metaphor for her retreat into her inner self. Translating becomes more difficult when these images are laden with emotion, as in 'A Minute's Silence' (p. 87), where the abandoned lover sees her rage reflected in the sky, the sea and the woods which are by turn 'zerkratzt' ('scratched'), 'zerwühlt' ('disordered') and 'zerzaust' ('tousled'). English does not have a prefix such as 'zer' to attach to verbs to indicate the extreme case. Here the translator has to resort to compensatory measures: by using 'scratched', 'scrunched up', and 'scruffy', the repetition of the initial 'scr' conveys some of the repetition in the original.

As a rule I tried to stay as close to Lange's syntax as English permits. I made only one exception – in the poem 'In My Dreams' (p. 65). In this poem the poet gives free rein to her imagination, in her dreams she is powerful and can fulfil ambitions which remain unfulfilled in her life. In German she uses the perfect tense and sets up a series of actions conveyed by the past participle in each instance. She uses the first person singular determiner 'I' only once explicitly in the first verse and three times in the second verse, although, of course, all the actions in the poem are hers. It is a poem of dramatic action. In English the omission of 'I' with the verb in the past tense resulted in what sounded like a series of random actions and the ultimate effect was to reduce the drama of the

German. I therefore inserted 'I' in (almost) every line. In order to retain some of the end rhymes, this meant introducing inversion, which is not usual in English but in this instance I would argue that it is justified since it maintains the dramatic action of the dream. One side-effect of this strategy was to introduce a masculine (grammatical) subject into the second verse where in German the male is very much an object, and not just a grammatical one:

> Ich habe ...
> den schönsten Ureinwohner genommen
> ein Kind bekommen.
> ...
>
> the most handsome native I desired
> a child he sired.

Here, again, the demands of the poetic form overrode other, arguably just as important, considerations.

The greatest challenge in poetry translation is to translate in such a way that both the potentiality of meanings and the linguistic nuances of the (in this case) German poem are available in the poem in the other language. The fact that this may be ultimately unattainable is not an argument for abandoning the translation project. On the contrary, it is a reason to produce more translations since each one will cumulatively contribute to a greater understanding of the poems in question.

Translation, especially translation of literature, is a never-ending story. As the first English translator of Sabine Lange's poetry, I hope I have opened a new chapter in Anglo-German poetic relations.

Jenny Williams 2005

INTRODUCTION

> ' ......On
> a frozen winter morning I come on my
> bicycle across the lake. Still
> virgin lies the thin covering of snow on the
> ice, and the horizon is like a backdrop made of
> grey woods and moon.'
> ('Fallada Archive')

Sabine Lange's poetry occupies that acceptable space within the canon of European writing which we like to call 'lyrical'. Such a definition is nowadays taken less seriously as an adjective with which to describe poetry; indeed Sabine Lange, in the delicately wrought collection *The Fishermen Sleep*, is treading a line that many English-language readers, writers and critics hesitate to approach. A recent trend in reviewing and criticism suggests that the lyric form is – as many have tried to assert with regard to the novel – 'dead', a thing of the past, redundant. The necessary impulse to experiment has created a sometimes bizarre and many-sided monster comprised of limbs of concrete poetry, 'confessional' poetry, and the equivalent of the pick 'n' mix bon-bon stall in the local supermarket: here a word, there a phrase, add a few line breaks, stitch in some pre-linguistic 'sounds' and convince yourself this is poetry.

But as several contemporary German, French and other poets on the European land mass have demonstrated, the lyric, by virtue of its deceptively delicate structure, its work in the labyrinth of the emotions, its historical habits of microscopic awareness of minutiae, remains the steely ennervated spine within the system of poetics we have inherited.

The lyric is that which we remember. It is the template out of which the *Iliad* and the *Odyssey* once sprang. It is part of our history and it's not going to disappear. And if the lyric is what we retain in memory, then it is also that which we pass on in germ form to infect the sensibilities of others.

Sabine Lange is a fine and vital poet whose work in the 1994 *Federchen Verlag* collection *Immer zu Fuß* has been translated under the title *The Fishermen Sleep* by Jenny Williams in a manner sensitive to the spirit of the German original and will undoubtedly appeal greatly to new readers. Lange was born in 1953 in Stralsund, then part of the German Democratic Republic. Music, mathematics and geography were the primary focus of her educational experience, in particular pianoforte, and she attended the Musikfernstudium at Rostock Konservatorium, later working as a freelance music tutor. Cofounder of the Hans-Fallada-Gesellschaft in Feldberg, she was based there as an archivist and published numerous articles, essays and independent works on the life and work of this novelist. Her poetry has been in print since 1987, with her first full collection appearing in 1994. It is to this that Jenny Williams has turned her attention as translator, capturing the sense of originality and the authentic voice that characterises Lange's work.

There is a pleasing absence of performance in this poetry: Lange is the observer within the landscape and against the backdrop of the seasons. Northernness, ice, wintry conditions bring a particular meditative beauty and interiority to the work. Her mood is sometimes peaceful, sometimes dark, often verging into an aloneness in which peace is not the precise note. But it never reads like the aloneness of disconnection.

Her subject is often love. Where it is to be found. How it strikes. What one must forgo in order to keep it. How to carry its weights and treacheries, or not. The poet is central yet not egocentral, and this is significant. In the best lyric poetry, egocentricity is absent although the self is being explored with the primal urges and symmetry of love often emerging as a dominant theme. We witness the approach of love, the momentous encounter, abandonment to love and a different abandonment in the wake of love. What follows then is the evolution of interesting notches of conciliation between self and the thing that is greater than self, where the poet seems to be released and healed through landscape and through ordinary habits of living. In the poem 'Letters' (p. 97) when the lover travels the world and writes to the speaker, she takes her letter-reading elsewhere, as in:

> and when I look at the sky
> I'm looking at the stars above him.

Earlier on though, the poet's unadorned language leads the reader straight into a dimension of experience that is creative and challenging. These are not 'easy' poems on a philosophical or psychological level. Nor are they love-poems *per se*, so much as poems of the landscape of attrition. The poet, one senses, is in love with beauty itself and each poem is created almost as a holding-receptacle for beauty. Beauty is revealed to be at the heart of things, as much as pain and dislocation. But at other times the poems are upbeat and at times funny and whimsical. In 'After a Shower of Rain' (p. 29), the poet takes on 'life in the raw', by drinking a glass 'with' herself: surely a celebration of renewal, of being in the fresh light of a post-shower moment. Other moods emerge when, in the poem 'Composure' (p. 35), she contemplates the presence of 'the time-eater', where a younger person refuses to be:

> ... swamped
> by the sum of your years
> and your foes ...
> not letting it silt up
> in the currents
> day after day.

Experiences register on several occasions in a tactile manner, sometimes when the poet is at a remove from what others are doing. The sensation – a slightly gothic one – occurs when she observes from a distance, whether outside a church, feeling 'the fists' of the organ in the nape of her neck, or observing a group of trees. Either way, with one notable exception, it's the response to a cluster, a crowd. In 'Rearview Mirror'(p. 77) though, a lover's look 'saws' into the nape of her neck. The imagery of cutting and destruction mounts as the journey continues. Knives, sharpened fingernails, hands like copper wire.

Yet the tone is exultant, the composition of each one often painterly. It is an embracing poetry that rejects cerebral games, and yet the instruction that the reader picks up is one of elevation, of high aesthetic values. As one would expect from Lange, (herself an experienced musician), the music-inspired poems introduce a different element. One listens *with* her as she eavesdrops on the church organist, secretly leaning 'for five minutes against his shoulder'. Yet neither music nor the other site of inspiration – landscape – are exactly divorced from the encounter with love. They function like redeeming chords that allow the writer to surface for air and to extend herself beyond the patterning she refers to as 'the enclosure of my soul'. Grieg, Sibelius, Chopin and Bach are part of her resistance armour, allowing her to unstop her own soul. That soul remaining open to the airs of life itself, Lange's vision is in one way neatly encapsulated in the following:

> 'My heart goes out to those besotted
> my words to those who have been forgotten
> my yearning to those travelling far and wide
> my love to those icing over inside'
> ('Four Maxims', p. 61)

Sensitivity and risk distinguish Jenny Williams's translations, ensuring that the poems are as compelling in English as they are in German. The risk comes from her decision to invert certain lines just as in the original German. Inversion can sound dated to English-language readers, a legacy of nineteenth-century poetic styles, but inversion is tonally and rhythmically correct in contemporary German, and Williams has reflected this in her lucid translations. Sometimes, she chooses end-rhyme at the expense of contemporary English syntax ('Evening Stillness in Feldberg', p. 65), and that too is effective. It is part of a good translator's refusal to write their own poem at the expense of the original.

Jenny Williams's utterly respectful translations are true to the measure of Sabine Lange's poetics, revealing the rhythms and tones of the originator's distinctive voice and conveying these with enormous skill. The poems are accessible yet complex and foreign, in the very best sense of that word.

Mary O'Donnell 2005

THE FISHERMEN SLEEP
DIE FISCHER SCHLAFEN

WINDFREUND

Endenovemberregen
Briefe sind angekommen
in denen nichts steht.
Und wieder zurückverwiesen
auf mich
hab ich mich angenommen
und brüderlich
den Wind gegrüßt
der vor dem Fenster blättert
und ich will lesen
wie er liest
und wettern wie er

DIE WINTER

Manchmal
kam Liebe zu mir
für ein großes Schiff
öffnete ich die Brücke
ein Holzspänchen
schwamm hindurch,
schwapp.

WINDFRIEND

Endofnovemberrain
letters have arrived for me
only empty leaves.
And turned down and back once more upon
myself
I have accepted me
and like a brother
greeted the wind
which sends leaves flying outside my window
I want to pick and choose
like he does
and storm like him

THE WINTERS

Sometimes
love came to me
for a great ship
I opened the bridge
a wood splinter
swam through,
splosh.

IN DER ERSTBESTEN ETÜDE VON CHOPIN

Daß ich hier so still sitzen kann, alle Welt abstreife wie einen löchrigen Socken, daß ich hier so meine Tage verbraten kann, als hätt ich sie fuderweise in der Scheuer, daß ich mich Ostern wirklich mit Osterwasser wasche und fortschwimme in der erstbesten Etüde von Chopin an alle Ufer, die mir dabei auswachsen, daß ich abends im Holzschuppen gespenstisch lache, wenn plötzlich die Petroleumlampe ausgeht, daß die Petroleumlampe nichts weiter als ein nostalgischer Wunsch ist von mir, auf den ich gern verzichten kann, daß ich überhaupt auf alles verzichten kann und während ich das denke, genußvoll die Augen schließe und die Augen gar nicht mehr öffne, weil etwas sie mir von innen zuhält, wie eine Tür, aus der ich nicht mehr hinaus soll, und ich stemme mich gegen die Tür und endlich, endlich komm ich nicht mehr fort.

IN THE NEXT BEST ÉTUDE BY CHOPIN

That I can sit so still here, cast off the whole
world like a stocking full of holes, that I can
fritter away my days here, as if
I had cartloads of them in the barn, that I
really wash myself at Easter with Easter milk
and swim away in the next best *étude*
by Chopin to all the shores which rise to meet
me, that in the evenings in the
wood shed I laugh eerily when
suddenly the petroleum lamp goes out, that the
petroleum lamp is nothing more than a
nostalgic desire of mine which I can
willingly forgo, that I can indeed
forgo everything and while I'm
thinking this, voluptuously close my eyes and
never open these eyes again because something
inside keeps them closed, like a door, through which
I shall never return, and I put my
weight against the door and at last, at last,
there is no escape.

MEIN SCHUH

Morgens begegne ich immer den
Ameisen sie erwarten nicht
daß ich grüße und so sind
wir schon eins.

Einige trete ich tot wahrscheinlich
mitten in der Arbeit und die Alten
halten Rat abseits
unter einem kleinen modrigen Holz.

Was sollen sie tun gegen meinen
Schuh und sie vermessen bei Nacht
seinen Abdruck und schreiben Essays
über den Tod und sterben

bei ihrer Lesung
wahrscheinlich mitten auf meinem Weg.

TERRASSE

Vor die Füße
fielen mir da zwei Hornissen
ein surrender Klumpen der
Sekunden wild kreiselte und
auseinanderschoß, eine
gegen mein Bein, ich saß auf einem
weißen Gartenstuhl nie fortgehen
dachte ich gerade selbstvergessen
den Blick durch die Bäume
fuhr auf
rannte ohne Atem was kannste

MY SHOE

In the mornings I encounter the
ants they do not expect me
to exchange greetings and so
we're agreed.

Some of them I most likely tread to death
in the midst of their work and the elders
hold counsel nearby
under a little piece of rotting wood.

What on earth should they do about my
shoe and they measure by night
its imprint, write papers and essays
about life and death and die

reading them
most likely right in my path.

ON THE TERRACE

At my feet there
landed two hornets
a buzzing ball that
for a few seconds rolled wildly
then shot apart, one
on to my leg, I was sitting on
a white garden chair never leave here
I was thinking quite lost to the world
looking through the trees
jumped up
took to my heels, nothing else for it

FALLADA-ARCHIV

Inmitten der Bäume steht meine Hütte.
Dach über die Stunden meines Tages. Am gefrorenen Wintermorgen komme ich mit dem Fahrrad über den See gefahren. Noch unberührt ist die dünne Schneedecke auf dem Eis, und der Horizont gleicht einer Kulisse aus Grauwald und Mond.
Knirschend zeichnet mein Fahrrad eine verräterische Spur. Sie führt direkt auf ein Haus zu. Es liegt etwas erhöht zwischen Büschen und Bäumen. Dieses Haus beherbergt das Werk eines Dichters.
Ich habe schon oft versucht, es zu beschreiben.
Als ich an diesem Morgen über den See fuhr, dachte ich, heute gelingt es mir.

NACH EINEM REGEN

Als ich meinen Mantel auszog
stieg ich aus meiner Haut
warf die Jahresringe
über die leeren Flaschen auf dem Tisch
öffnete die Fensterläden
zapfte den Regen von den Bäumen
und trank mit mir ein Glas

auf das nackte Leben

FALLADA ARCHIVE

In the midst of the trees stands my den.
Roof over the hours of my day. On
a frozen winter morning I come on my
bicycle across the lake. Still
virgin lies the thin covering of snow on the
ice, and the horizon is like a backdrop made of
grey woods and moon.
Crunching a path my bicycle leaves
a tell-tale trail. It leads directly to a
villa. A little elevated among
bushes, shrubs and trees, this villa houses
the work of a writer.
In the past I have often tried to
describe it.
As I was cycling across the lake this morning,
I'd a feeling I'd succeed today.

AFTER A SHOWER OF RAIN

As I took off my coat
I stepped out of my skin
threw the rings of the years
over the empty bottles on the table
opened the shutters
drew a measure of rain from the trees
and drank a glass with myself

to life in the raw

MORGENS

Lauft nur, Rehe
lauft nur davon
mißtraut mir

sicherer sind wahrlich
die nebligen Wiesen
das braune Schilf

dahin ich selbst
laufen werde

TOCCATA

Tonleitern
hängen wie Faultiere
zwischen meinen gespreizten Fingern
während ich nach der ganzen Welt
greifen möchte früher
hat mir Johann Sebastian die Finger
massiert bis hoch
in die Schultern und manchmal was
Pastorales in mein Ohr
geflüstert ich bin
keines seiner zwanzig Kinder
geworden doch heute
klopf ich den Staub aus den Fugen
gebe den Faultieren
einen Schreckschuß in d-moll
und greife nach
der ganzen Welt

IN THE MORNING

Run away, deer,
run away now
don't trust me

safer are verily
the misty meadows
the brown reeds

where I myself
shall run to

TOCCATA

Scales
are suspended like sloths
between my splayed fingers
while I want to reach out and touch
the whole world once
Johann Sebastian massaged my fingers
right up to my
shoulders and sometimes he whispered
pastorally into
my ear one of his
twenty children I have not
become but today
I beat the dust out of the fugues
address to the sloths a
warning shot in D minor
and reach out and touch
the whole world

BEGINNENDE TROPFEN

Abends trommelt der Regen
gegen mein Fenster
erinnert mich an deine nervösen Hände
deine ewig bewegten Hände, Regenhände
mit den weichen Kuppen
am Nagelbett wie beginnende
Tropfen
die nicht aufhören können
an mein Fenster zu trommeln ...

fünf rinnen mir ins Hemd
als mit einem Windstoß
das Glas zerspringt

THE FIRST DROPS

In the evening the rain drums
against my window
my thoughts run to your nervous hands
your agitated, restless hands, rain hands
with their soft tips
on nailbeds like the first
drops
which cannot stop
drumming on my window...

five run down inside my shirt
as with a gust of wind
the glass shatters

GELASSENHEIT

Für dich
bin ich herzoffen
du lebst
als wäre
der Zeitfresser ein Insekt
und du ein Insektenfresser
die Gewißheit
steht in deinem Gesicht
ganz still und gelassen
du bist jung
weil du bestehst
auf jenen angeborenen Instinkt
du selbst zu sein
läßt ihn nicht zuschütten
von der Zahl deiner Jahre
und Feinde
läßt ihn nicht verkümmern
im Bleichlicht einer
kränkelnden Sonne
läßt ihn nicht versanden
im Planierwind
Tag um Tag.

COMPOSURE

For you
my heart is open
you live
as if the
time-eater were an insect
and you were an insect-eater
assuredness
is written on your face
quite calm and composed
you are young
because you insist
on that innate instinct
to be yourself
not letting it be swamped
by the sum of your years
and your foes
not letting it waste away
in the bleaching glare
of a sickly sun
not letting it silt up
in the currents
day after day.

DAUERFROST

Der Dauerfrostboden
reicht von Äquator
zu Äquator
wenn wir fallen
schlagen unsere Körper hart auf
unser Blut versickert nicht
und roter Schleim umhüllt
den Erdball
wie eine neue Sphäre
in der sich kein Chlorophyll
mehr bildet
für unsere
grünen Kopfkissen

PERMAFROST

The permafrosted earth
stretches from equator
to equator
when we fall
our bodies crack open on impact
our blood does not seep away
and a red slime envelops
the globe
like a new spherical orb
in which no chlorophyll
forms any more
for our
green pillows

ERNTE 86

Laß uns
einander ernten
wir stehen gut
im Gift

Faß mich an
mit trockenen Händen
und küsse mich
durch eine

Abwaschbare Folie
wir wollen uns lieben
wie Adam und Eva
nur nicht so feucht

In Worten ist alles
erlaubt nur auch
beim Sprechen bitte
nicht spucken

Am besten Rücken
an Rücken und keine
Tabus so wolln
wir uns lieben
und ganz antiseptisch
pflücken

HARVEST 86

Let us
harvest each other
we're ready
for cutting

Touch me
with hands that are dry
and kiss me
through

Some easy-wipe wrapping
we'll make love together
just like Adam and Eve
but not as damp

In words everything is
allowed just please
when you're speaking
don't spit

Best of all is back
to back and without any
taboos that's how
to love each other
and antiseptically
pick each other

VERGEBLICH

Finden nicht
so schnell wir auch suchen
immer eiliger
immer verschwitzter

der sanfte Akkord
einer Gitarre
schläft in meinem Mund
das wär eine schöne Sprache
könnten wir reden

doch wir müssen essen
sieh die vielen Zähne
die meterlangen Därme
draus

knüpft die Erde den Strick sich

IN VAIN

Cannot find
however fast we seek
ever more speedily
ever more feverishly

the gentle chord
of a guitar
sleeps in my mouth
that would be a lovely language
if we could speak

but we have to eat
look at all the teeth
the metres of intestine
from which

the earth ties a noose for itself

GEDANKE

... wenn alles
vor die Hunde geht
die großen Weltenkuchen zerbrechen
die Rosinen herausfallen
und ganze Völker erschlagen
die Meere gären und Schwung holen
die Winde ihre Kraft zusammenlegen
bleibt der Einzeller Gedanke
hofft
daß Geist Seele und Fleisch
sich vermählen in guter Sekunde
und Licht
auf einen neuen Weg fällt
an dessen Ende
keine Zielgerade mehr
zur tödlichen Eile treibt.

THOUGHT

... when every
thing goes to the dogs
the great world cakes crumble
and out the raisins tumble
and whole nations slaughter
the oceans begin to seethe and pound
the winds their powers combine
there remains the single-cell organism thought
hopes
that spirit, soul and flesh
are wedded at a good moment
and light
falls on a new way
at the end of which
no finishing strait
spurs on to deadly haste.

***

Am Baum
das Auto war
wie zusammengeknülltes Silberpapier

das man nur
fortwerfen brauchte
aus dieser unbewegten Landschaft

mit Kastanien
gelben Feldern
roten Dächern

und den Wolken
die sichtbar
ein Tempo vorgeben

LEBEN MIT DER SCHNEESCHIPPE

Die mir den Weg freihält.
Die vor der Tür steht und nicht klingelt,
sondern taktvoll wartet.
Die immer für mich da ist. Die nie den Kopf
in den Sand steckt und daher keinerlei Fragen
aufwirft. Nur Schnee. Zu einem großen
Haufen. Und ich springe hinein, ha!
Und bin wieder Kind.

***

Against the tree
the car was
like scrunched up silver paper

that just needed
to be removed
from this impassive landscape

with chestnut trees
yellow fields
red roofs

and the clouds
which clearly
set a speed limit

LIFE WITH THE SNOW SHOVEL

Which clears the way for me.
Which stands at the door and does not ring,
but waits tactfully.
Which is always there for me. Which never sticks
its head in the sand and therefore throws up no
questions. Just snow. In a big
pile. And I jump in, ah!
And am a child again.

SONNTAGS

... belausche ich Gottesdienste
aus solcher Entfernung
wo nur noch das Raunen
der Predigt
durch die eisenbeschlagene Tür
an mein Ohr dringt
ich will gar nichts verstehen
keine Weisheit aufschnappen
nur die Geborgenheit fühlen
die man in der Nähe
einer friedlichen
und beseelten Menschenansammlung
empfängt –
und die Fäuste der Orgel
in meinem Nacken verspüren.

MAN SAGT

Dabei bin ich
noch jung und alle Türen
wie man sagt
stehn mir offen
doch es ist
wie im Traum und man träumt
daß man geht
und geht kaum

ON SUNDAYS

... I listen to Church services
from such a distance
that only the droning
of the sermon
through the heavy iron-clad door
reaches my ear
I don't want to understand
catch a word of wisdom
just feel the comfort and the warmth
which the proximity
of a peaceful
and harmonious human gathering
bestows –
and feel the fists of the organ
in the nape of my neck.

THEY SAY

But I'm
still young and all doors
as they say
are open to me
yet it is
as in a dream when you dream
you're moving
and hardly move at all

EINFACHE BEWEGUNG

Zuweilen ziehe ich meine Hände
aus dem Gewäsch der Welt
wie aus einer Schüssel Lauge
schüttle den ätzenden Schaum
von den Handrücken Gischt
der geifernden Münder
und lasse die Hände einfach
in die Hosentaschen gleiten
ganz unauffällig so
wie ein Diebesgut

***

Igelstunden
Spiegelwunden
alles rollt sich ein
Ich seh meine blassen Augen
und muß freundlich sein

A SIMPLE MOVEMENT

At times I take my hands
out of the hogwash of the world
like out of a bucket of slops
shake the caustic scum off the
back of my hands the spray
of the slobbering mouths
and simply slip my hands
into my trouser pockets
quite unobtrusively
like stolen goods

***

Hedgehog seasons
mirror lesions
everything curls into a ball
I look at my pale pale eyes
and must be kind to all

BÄUME

Wenn ich aus dem Fenster sehe, sehe ich Bäume.
Wenn ich mich wegdrehe und nicht hinaussehe, spüre ich in meinem Nacken: Bäume. Dann brechen sie lautlos, bündeln sich zu großen Packen, ebensolche wie sie von den sibirischen Wäldern auf der Angara zum Meer hintreiben, und legen sich auf meine Schulter.
Auf der Angara singt ein Flößer und fängt Lachse. Er springt von Floß zu Floß und wirft seine Angel aus. Dann erreicht er mein Ohr, hängt seinen Drilling ein und sagt: Heut beißen sie nicht.
Dann schließe ich die Fensterläden.

TREES

When I look out of the window, I'm looking at
Trees.
When I turn away and do not
look out, I feel in the nape of my neck:
Trees. Then they break off noiselessly, converge
into timber rafts, like the ones which float
on the Angara from the Siberian forests
down to the sea, and they come to rest
on my shoulders.
On the Angara a raftsman sings and catches
salmon. He jumps from raft to raft and casts
out his fishing line. Then he reaches my ear,
attaches his fish-hook and says: They're
not biting today.
Then I close the shutters.

***

Abends,
wenn ich meine vier Wände
um mich geschart habe
den Tisch in leichte Schräglage gebracht
daß es scheint immer kommt mir etwas
entgegen flieht von mir weg
und als könnte alles jederzeit kippen
daß ich nicht bleiben muß
im gerade eingenommenen Zustand
der sich daran macht
mich zu verfertigen abzutöten
daß ich also dem Tod
immer wieder entgeh
abends,
wenn ich meine vier Wände
um mich geschart habe

FRAGMENT

Bin Fragment
nett angefang'n
und nicht zu End

ein Stückl Bruch
von einem Ganz
der Meister ging zu früh

zum Tanz

***

In the evenings,
when I have gathered
my four walls around me
arranged the table at a slight angle
so that it seems something is always
coming towards fleeing from me
and everything could collapse any time
so that I don't have to stay
in the position I've just adopted
which is now trying
to mould me kill me off
so that I thus again and
again elude death
in the evenings,
when I have gathered
my four walls around me

FRAGMENT

I'm a fragment
nicely begun
and not quite done

a tiny piece
of a great whole
the sculptor left early

to rock 'n' roll

KATZE

Eben habe ich mich vor den Ofen gelegt,
mich gekrümmt wie eine Katze und dabei
eine Chopin-Etüde gehört.
Ich hatte Augen so grün wie Katzenaugen,
meine Krallen kratzten verspielt über den
Läufer, und mein Fell sträubte sich und wurde
wieder weich, ich schloß behaglich die Augen.
Als eine Kohle im Ofen brach, und ich wußte,
daß es weiter nichts ist als eine Kohle, war ich
auf einmal wieder Mensch, und ich erschrak.

CAT

I had just lain down in front of the hearth,
had curled up like a cat and was
listening to one of Chopin's études.
I had eyes as green as cats' eyes,
my claws scratched playfully over the
fireside rug, and my fur bristled and became
soft again, contentedly I closed my eyes.
When a piece of coal crackled in the fire and I knew
that it was only a piece of coal, I suddenly
became human again, and took fright.

ZAUNGAST

Der Orgelspieler hat aufgehört
durch welche Kirchentür
wird er kommen
durch die kleine Seitentür
durch die große Haupttür
wird er den Schlüssel leise drehen
wird das Schloß schnappen
wird er mich ansehen
wird er durch mich hindurchsehen
ich habe ihm heimlich zugehört
fünf Minuten an seiner Schulter gelehnt
wird er mich mürrisch ansehen
durch welche Kirchentür wird er kommen
(warum eigentlich er?)
soll ich lieber fortgehen
oder wie ein zufälliger Spaziergänger
vorübergehen
eben hör ich das Schloß leise schnappen
welches war es
das von der großen Haupttür
das von der kleinen Seitentür
keine öffnet sich
der Orgelspieler hat aufgehört
erschrocken geh ich schnell fort.

EAVESDROPPER

The organist has stopped playing
through which door of the church
will he come
through the little side door
through the great main door
will he turn the key very softly
will the lock click shut
will he look at me
will he look through me
I listened to him secretly
I leaned for five minutes against his shoulder
will he look sullenly at me
through which door of the church will he come
(why he of all people?)
perhaps I ought to leave
or like some one out for an afternoon stroll
casually pass by
I've just heard the lock click softly shut
which one was it
the lock of the great main door
the lock of the little side door
neither door opens
the organist has stopped playing
I take fright and quickly depart.

IN EINE DECKE GEHÜLLT

In eine Decke gehüllt
immer dieselbe Platte hören
Grieg wahrscheinlich
wahrscheinlich Sibelius
streichelnder abweisender Norden
dessen Bäume sich häuten
heimlich im Nebel

daß ich schreiben kann
auf diese leblose Schlangenhaut ich lebe
so versprühe ich mich
gegen die große Walze
die unaufhörlich rollt
und wehre mich gegen die Einfriedung
meiner Seele
erkläre den Krieg
der harmlosesten Verallgemeinerung

WEGE

Das Leben verliert sich
in scheinbaren Wegen
gut asphaltiert und
ausgeschildert –
besser
man läuft quer in den Wald
und wildert und läßt
sich von Gräsern und
Zweigen berühren
sucht Wege
die unter der Haut
entlang führen

WRAPPED UP IN A BLANKET

Wrapped up in a blanket
always listening to the same record
Grieg most likely
most likely Sibelius
the caressing repelling North
whose trees shed their skins
mysteriously in the mist

so that I can write
on this lifeless snake skin I live
and so I spray my pen
against the steam roller
which keeps on rolling
and resist the enclosure
of my soul
declare outright war
on the most harmless generalization

PATHS

Life loses itself in
what appear to be paths
well tarmacked and
signposted –
better
to run off to the forest
and forage and enjoy
the caresses of
grasses and branches
to seek paths
which lead along
under the skin

GRUSS

Den Lebendigen mein Gruß
die da kochen und backen und
Kinder aufziehen
die das Gewimmel des Lebens
ausmachen
wovon die Wärme aufsteigt
wovon der Himmel so blau wird
und das Wasser so blau
einsam sind die Schreiber
in ihren Hütten
stillverdrossen grau
und ungenau

VIER WORTE

Mein Herz gehört den Besessenen
meine Worte sind für die Vergessenen
meine Sehnsucht gehört den Reisenden
meine Liebe den langsam Vereisenden

A GREETING

I salute the living
who are cooking and baking and
bringing up children
who make up
the hustle and bustle of life
which gives rise to the warmth
which makes the sky so blue
so blue the water
solitary are the scribes
in their dens
silently melancholy
grey and shadowy

FOUR MAXIMS

My heart goes out to those besotted
my words to those who have been forgotten
my yearning to those travelling far and wide
my love to those icing over inside

BOHNENWERDER

Hinter den Hügeln
da liegt meine Weide
da bin ich Kuh und Schaf zugleich
da bin ich geborgen und kann
mich versorgen mit Gras
und Wasser vom Teich

Hinter den Hügeln
da wohnt meine Freude
und das Gras wächst für mich nur allein
da lern ich laufen und lachen
und saufen da bin ich
Pferd und Schwein

Hinter den Hügeln
verbring ich die Tage
die es noch gar nicht gibt
und in den Nächten hinter den Hügeln
bin ich in ein Märchen
verliebt

THE BOHNENWERDER ISLAND

Hidden beyond the hills
you will find my pasture
there I am both cow and sheep
there I feel protected and can
feed myself on grass and
water from the deep

Hidden beyond the hills
you will find my delight
and the grass grows just for me of course
there I learn to leap and laugh
and feast there I am both
pig and horse

Hidden beyond the hills
I spend all the days
which have not yet been
and in the nights hidden beyond the hills
I am in love with
a dream

IM TRAUM

Im Traum
hab ich eine Straße verlegt
ein paar Bäume gesägt
ein Zelt aufgeschlagen
Tannenzapfen zusammengetragen
Hölzer zur Flamme gerieben
eine Herde Schafe ins Tal getrieben

Ich habe den See in Flaschen gefüllt
wie ein Löwe gebrüllt
den schönsten Ureinwohner genommen
ein Kind bekommen
ich hab es gehegt
im Traum
habe ich eine Straße verlegt

FELDBERGER ABENDSTILLE

Die kleinen Häuser schlafen ein
ein Hund bellt noch im Garten
zwei Äpfel fallen aus dem Baum
die Mondfrau legt die Karten

hinter den Fenstern gähnt man schon
im Kirchturm schlägt die Stunde
der See dreht seine Wasser um
die Liebe geht die Runde

IN MY DREAMS

In my dreams
a road I built
some trees I felled
a tent I pitched
pine cones I gathered
to light a fire some sticks I rubbed
a flock of sheep down from the hills I moved

The lake I into bottles poured
and like a lion roared
the most handsome native I desired
a child he sired
I cherished it
in my dreams
a road I built

EVENING STILLNESS IN FELDBERG

The little houses fall asleep
dogs bark in their back yards
two apples fall down from the tree
the woman in the moon reads the cards

behind the windows people yawn
the hour the church tower sounds
the lake churns up its waters
and love goes on its rounds

DER VORSICHTIGE

Der Vorsichtige wartet noch. Er wartet noch den nächsten Tag ab, setzt erst den Fuß auf das Eis, wenn schon die Motorräder der Jugendlichen darüber hinwegjagen. Der Vorsichtige wartet auch jetzt, er könnte in Fahrtrichtung geraten, auch könnte durch warme Strömungen das Eis ungleichmäßig gefroren sein und der böse Zufall hat es vielleicht gerade auf ihn abgesehen.
Der Vorsichtige ist literarisch gebildet, er weiß, daß Georg Heym als 25jähriger beim Eislaufen auf der Havel ertrank.
Der Vorsichtige führt eine Kartei von möglichen Schicksalsschlägen.
Er ist auf Vollständigkeit bedacht.

THE CAUTIOUS MAN

The cautious man prefers to wait. He prefers to wait
until the next day, does not set foot on
the ice until the motorbikes of the
young people are careering across it. The
cautious man even then prefers to wait: he might
end up in their path or warm currents could
even have caused the ice to freeze in an
irregular fashion and given his luck he
could be the next victim of chance.
The cautious man is well versed in literature, he knows
that Georg Heym at the age of 25 went skating on the
river Havel and drowned.
The cautious man keeps a catalogue of
possible pitfalls.
Comprehensiveness is his main concern.

BROT UND WEIN

Schon vor zehn Frühlingen
wollt ich mich verlieben
ein altes Versprechen
an mein langsam gewordenes
Herzpferd

doch in diesem März
wird ich es wohl endgültig
vor den Pflug spannen
und ihm den wilden Wein
zur Ader lassen

damit in den nächsten
zehn Frühlingen zumindest
das Brot noch gedeiht.

ZUSTAND

Wie Affen
von Urwaldbaum zu Urwaldbaum
hangeln wir
von Höhepunkt zu Höhepunkt
mit dem kleinen Unterschied
dazwischen
schweben wir nicht.

BREAD AND WINE

It was ten Springs ago
I aimed to fall in love
an old promise I made
to my now slow-paced
heart horse

but when this March comes
I think for one last time I'll
put him to the plough
and bleed the wild wine
from out of his veins

so that for the next
ten Springs to come at least
the bread will be plenteous.

CONDITION

Like monkeys
from jungle tree to jungle tree
we make our way
from high point to high point
with the one small difference
we don't hover
between them.

FASCHING

Er wollte zum Fasching, bekleidet mit seinem
dünnen Nervenkostüm schlotterte er durch die
enge Gasse. Ob man mich erkennt, überlegte
er, blieb unschlüssig stehen, zündete sich eine
Zigarette an und betrachtete die
Vorübergehenden: ... zwei Piraten, eine
Märchenfee, einen Leichenbestatter ... Sie
werden wissen, wo es ist, dachte er und
folgte ihnen.

VERBAND

du und ich
wir leben im Verband
der Bindewörter
nichtssagende und doch
verbindende
Sowohlalsauchs auf ewig
grammatischen Regeln
gehorchend stehen
wir zu beiden Seiten des
und

CARNIVAL

He wanted to join the carnival, dressed in his
thin suit of nerves he shivered and shook through the
narrow street. Will people recognize me, he wondered,
stopped, stood still uncertain, took out and lit a
cigarette and looked at the people
passing by: ... two pirates, a
fairy, an undertaker... They
are sure to know where it is, he thought, and
followed them.

CONJUNCTION

you and I
we live conjoined
by connectors
saying nothing and yet
connecting
Notonlybutalsos for ever
obeying grammatical rules
we stand
each on either side of
and

STILL-LEBEN

Die Tische des Schweigens
die Dreiertische am Abend

und immer dieselbe Wurst
sagt das Kind

und die Eltern schneiden
die Scheiben stumm

noch dünner als der Kaffee
sind die Worte

und das Kind spricht
mit vollem Mund

STILL-LIFE

The tables of silence
three at table every evening

and always the same salami
says the child

and the parents slice
the salami in silence

even weaker than the coffee
are the words

and the child speaks
with its mouth full

MÜDE GENUG

Müde genug wär ich
diese Liebe zurückzugeben
ans Amt für die Umverteilung
von Irrtümern

Lust hätt ich
meine Beine neu
ins Rennen zu schlagen
(ach was Kompressionsstrümpfe)

aber der Sand
im oberen
Trichter hat merklich
abgenommen

er ist mir zuweilen
in die Ohren geronnen
und ich höre nicht mehr

ob mein Herz noch
beschleunigen kann.

TIRED ENOUGH

I'm tired enough to
return this love to the
Office for the Redistribution
of Errors

I'd like to
enter my legs
in the race again
(to hell with support tights)

but the sand
in the top of
the timer has noticeably
reduced

it has on occasion
run into my ears and
I can't hear any more

if my heart can
beat any faster.

RÜCKSPIEGEL

In deinem Rückspiegel
bin ich am schönsten
weil ich davongehe
ich lasse dich
ich fasse mich
und halte die Schritte im Takt –

dein Blick sägt
meinen Nacken ein
es ist
die intensivste Berührung
die du mir je
geschenkt hast

AUFSTIEG

Auf der Haut
der Würgegriff
deiner Worte

die verborgenen Messer
deiner Blicke
gehe ich

mit gekrümmten Zehen
die Scherben
hinauf

REARVIEW MIRROR

In your rearview mirror
I am loveliest
because I am going
I leave you
I come to
and keep my steps in time –

your look saws
into the nape of my neck
it is
the most intensive contact
you have ever
granted me

ASCENT

On my skin
the stranglehold
of your words

the hidden knives
of your looks
I walk

with curled toes
up the
splinters

UND ES UNS FORTTREIBT ...

Wenn wir schon leicht gefächert sind
in den Augenwinkeln und guten
Wind in die Sicht bekommen
jedenfalls einen der schon manches
bewegt hat
und jetzt das bunte Herbstlaub
aufscheucht daß uns
die Lust zu tanzen ankommt oder
das gleichmäßige Frösteln
über die Haut geht
und es uns forttreibt
wieder nach Wärme noch immer
nach Wärme ...

BRUNNEN

Rissig die Haut, Borke
unter deiner Hand

widerborstig das Haar
gegen deins

Stolpergestein überall,
welche Unordnung

so fallen wir abermals
einander in die Brunnen.

AND IT DRIVES US ON....

When we have begun to crumple
in the corners of our eyes and a fair
wind comes into view
at least one which has already caused
quite a stir
and now whips up the brightly coloured
autumn leaves so that
the desire to dance overcomes us
or that constant shivering
creeps over our skin
and it drives us on
once more in search of warmth still on
in search of warmth...

WISHING WELLS

Rough my skin, bark
to your touch

unruly my hair
against yours

nothing but obstacles
what a shambles

and so we fall once more
into each other's wells.

SAFARI

Wenn du dann eingeschlafen bist hinterm
Steuer und über die Autobahn rast und von
einer galoppierenden Herde Zebras träumst,
nur vage und durchbrochen von dunkel-
nächtlichem Grasland, wenn du dann
eingeschlafen bist, lege ich meine Wange an
deine Schulter und schließe beruhigt die
Augen, schwinge mich mit dir auf eines der
Zebras, um dem Löwen zu entkommen, der
schon hungrig hinter einem Gebüsch lauert ...

DOCH AUS MEINEM GESICHT

Ich habe dich nicht gehalten
und du bist freigekommen

alles ist gewonnen
alles verloren

die Straßen behalten ihre Namen
und der Regen sein Geräusch

ich behalte meinen Mantel
und meine Schuh

doch aus meinem Gesicht
sind dreizehn Blicke gewichen

und sieben Sprachen
aus meinem Blut

SAFARI

When you have fallen asleep at the
wheel and are racing along the motorway and
dreaming of a galloping herd of zebras,
only dimly and interspersed with the dark
night of the grassland, when you have
fallen asleep, I rest my cheek on
your shoulder and reassured I close my
eyes, swing myself up with you onto one of the
zebras, in order to escape the lion which
is lying hungrily in wait behind a bush...

BUT FROM MY FACE

I did not keep hold of you
and you cut free

all has been won
all lost

the streets keep hold of their names
and the rain its refrain

I keep hold of my coat
and my shoes

but from my face
thirteen looks have drained

and seven languages
from my blood

RÜCKZUCK

Heut bin ich einem Einsamen
durchs Haar gefahren
mit dem Draht meiner Hände
und kupfernem Blick
er konnt nicht erkennen
ob ich ihn kämme
oder nun liebe
und zuckte zurück

STÖRUNG

Dieser Juliabend
wär ein Gefäß für uns
jemand hat es umgestülpt
wir gelangen nicht hinein

könnten wir uns
an die Henkel hängen
wie zwei fröhliche Affen

stattdessen
ziehen wir schweigend davon
jeder in seine Zuflucht

JUMP START

Today with the wire of my hands
and a copper look
I ran through the hair
of a solitary man
he couldn't tell
if I was combing him
or now love him
and jumped back with a start

INTERRUPTION

This July evening
could be a vessel for us
some one turned it upside down
now there's no way in

if only we could
swing on the handles
like two merry monkeys

but instead
we silently move on
each to our own hideaway

APFELSPRUCH

Wart nicht
bis die Äpfel bräunen
iß sie frisch
vom Apfeltisch

Gib dem Liebsten
einen ungeschnittnen
weißen soll
er sich verbeißen

Bis du kommst
mit reifren Früchten
oder anderen
Ausflüchten

STEILUFER

Fremder Schöner
wie gern Schönfremder
würd ich durch dein Blut
mal schwimmen
es ist ja Sommer
der wievielte von hinten –

könnten wir zählen
wir legten das Ruder
die himmlischste Weile
ans Ufer das Ufer
es stieg uns
unendlich
zu Kopf

APPLE PROVERB

Don't wait
until the apples rot
eat them fresh
from the dish

Give your loved one
an uncut white one
let him
chew on it

Till you bring
him a riper crop
or some other
sop

STEEP BANK

Strange handsome man
how handsome stranger
I'd love to swim
through your blood
it's summer you know
how many are left –

if we could count
we would rest the oars
for a heavenly while
on the bank the bank
it would go
immeasurably
to our heads

SPASS

du hast mir Spaß gemacht
mit dir hab ich gelacht
daß sich ein Balken bog
in unserm Hungertrog

wir hungerten nach Liebe
und hatten das Gefäß
egal, auf wen ichs schiebe
Sex ist ja zeitgemäß

wir machtens auf die Schnelle
und schwammen auf der Welle
daß Innigkeit nur stört

hast du mir zugehört?

GEDENKMINUTE

Heut ist der Himmel zerkratzt
von spitzen Fingernägeln
greint deine Geliebte,
Liebster?

Und das Meer ist zerwühlt
liegt wie eine unordentliche Decke am Strand
wütet dein Schatz, Darling?

Und der Wald ist zerzaust
wie manchmal dein Haar
als ich es noch war ...

... im Wald, im Meer, himmlisch ...

GOOD TIMES

I've had good times with you
we've laughed so much we two
that we nearly burst
the bubble of our thirst

it was for love we thirsted
and had the wherewithal
so with the tide we drifted
for Sex was topical

we did it at great speed
and feelings – we agreed –
just get in the way

do you hear a word I say?

A MINUTE'S SILENCE

Today the heavens are scratched
by sharpened fingernails
is your loved one wailing,
Beloved?

And the sea is scrunched up
and lies like a crumpled blanket on the beach
is your treasure seething, Darling?

And the woods are scruffy
as sometimes your hair
when I was the one...

... in the woods, in the sea, heavenly...

GESAGT

Nun wandere ich weiter,
dich habe ich genommen wie eine Festung
und dich wie eine Kleckerburg am Strand
und dich habe ich ausgenommen wie eine
Weihnachtsente
und dich habe ich eingenommen wie eine
Droge
nun wandere ich weiter, trunken
die Festungsmauer im Nacken, den Strandsand
zwischen den Zähnen und eine Rosine im Hirn.

WENN DU EINE LIEBE HAST ...

Wenn du eine Liebe hast, stelle sie nicht ins
Vertiko, zu den Sektgläsern aus Kristall, dem
guten Bavaria-Porzellan, lege sie nicht in die
Mappe mit den Urkunden und
Versicherungsabschlüssen, auch nicht zur
schläfrigen Katze auf die Ofenbank, wenn du
eine Liebe hast, schlage das Tuch um die
Schultern und gehe vor die Stadt, dorthin, wo
die Müllhalden in die Wiesen münden und die
Wiesen in den Wald und der Wald in den
Himmel und der Himmel in den Wind, der dir
das Tuch von den Schultern nimmt ...

PAST AND PRESENT

And so I carry on my way,
you I took like a fortress
and you like a sandcastle on the beach
and you I took apart like a Christmas goose
and you I took in like a drug
and so I carry on my way, inebriated
the fortress wall in the back of my neck, the sand
between my teeth and stardust in my eyes.

WHEN YOU HAVE A LOVE ...

When you have a love, don't stand it in
the china cabinet with the crystal champagne glasses, the
good Bavaria china, don't put it in the
folder with the certificates and
insurance policies, nor beside the
sleepy cat on the hearthside rug either, when you
have a love, throw your scarf around your
shoulders and go out of town to where
the rubbish tip meets the meadows and the
meadows the woods and the woods the
sky and the sky the wind, which
takes the scarf from off your shoulders...

SCHNEIDEGRAS

Immer zwischen den Zeitungen
die täglichen
Dienstbriefe
mit den scharfen Rändern
Schneidegras,
Dünnbriefe mit glattblättrigen
Broschüren Einladungen
zu Veranstaltungen
auf Diskette

das Herzauge
entbindet die Sehkraft
als ein Kuvert
mit deiner Tinte
aus der Zeitung fällt

CUTTING GRASS

Always among the newspapers
the daily
business letters
with their sharp edges
cutting grass,
thin letters with smooth leaved
brochures, invitations
to events
on disk

my heart's eye
is quickened when it sees
an envelope
addressed in your ink
drop out of the newspaper

LIEBESGEDICHT

Dich könnt ich
lieben die Möglichkeit
ins Bild gesetzt raubt mir
die Sinne übersteigt meine
schönsten Träume
stockt mir den Atem treibt den Tod
in die Berge and den Wind
aus dem Ärmel immer ein
Kunststück liegt überall bereit
ein Straußenei eine Taube die
sich weiterverwandelt bis
man nichts mehr erkennen kann
als das berstende Weiß
vor Augen das
hinter der letzten Tür

LOVE POEM

You I could
love imagining the
possibility robs me
of my senses exceeds my
loveliest dreams
takes my breath away drives death
into the hills and the wind
always and everywhere a
a work of art at the ready
an ostrich egg a dove which
keeps transforming itself until
you can see nothing more
than the exploding white
before your eyes
beyond the final door

KAUFHAUS

Es ist
als wenn ich dich
im Gewühl verloren hätte
im Kaufhausgewühl
ich bleibe an dem Stand
wo wir zuletzt zusammenwaren

Während du schon
zwischen den Lampen
im dritten Stock klirrst
süchtig nach neuem Licht
das die unsagbare Sehnsucht ausbrennt
warte ich
bis dein rastloser Körper
auf die Rolltreppe fällt
die vor meinen Füßen
ihre letzte Station macht

Ich werde nicht
zu dir niederknien
obwohl mein Stolz es zuließe
ansehen werde ich dich
von dem Stand aus
wo wir zuletzt zusammenwaren

DEPARTMENT STORE

It is
as if I
had lost you in the crush
the crush of a department store
I remain at the point
where we last stood together

While you are
tinkling among the lamps
on the third floor
craving a new light
to extinguish the inexpressible longing
I wait
until your restless body
falls onto the escalator
which comes to a final halt
at my feet

I shall not
kneel down to you
although my pride would permit it
I shall observe you
from the point
where we last stood together

BERÜHRUNG

Der sog die Leere aus mir
als wärs eine Speise
und gebrauchte noch eine
Serviette daß ich endgültig glaubte
er hätte was
zu sich genommen
und gewann wieder
ein schönes Stück
Teppich unter die Füße
daß ich plötzlich aufstehn
lächeln und in die Küche
gehen konnte und ganz normal
vielleicht sogar zärtlich
willst'n Bier fragen ...

BRIEFE

Einer fährt durch die Welt, von Land zu Land
und schreibt mir Briefe, ich sitze
auf einem Baumstumpf und ordne sie
chronologisch, löse die Briefmarken ab
und ordne sie geographisch
dann lese ich die Briefe noch und noch
einmal
und verschließe zwischen Baum und
Borke,
währenddessen fährt er durch die Welt
und schreibt mir Briefe
und wenn ich den Himmel seh,
seh ich die Sterne über ihm.

CONTACT

He sucked the void out of me
as if it was a meal
went as far as using a
serviette so that I actually thought
he had indeed
had something to eat
and feeling again
a nice piece of
carpet under my feet
I could suddenly get up
smile and go into the kitchen
and ask quite normally
perhaps even tenderly
woodcha like a beer...

LETTERS

A man travels the world, from land to land
and writes letters to me, I sit
on a tree stump and put them into
chronological order, remove the stamps
and put them into geographical order,
then I read the letters and read them one
more time
and conceal them between tree and
bark,
and all the while he travels the world
and writes letters to me
and when I look at the sky
I'm looking at the stars above him.

KOMMUNIKATION

Wie intellektuell
wir reden
dabei möchte ich
mit dir
in einen hohlen Baum kriechen und

Verstecken wir uns also
in einem hohlen Kopf

ALLE BOOTE

In die Jazz-Keller gehe ich
wegen des Sängers Lippen
wegen des Sängers Kehle
wo sich was bewegt
lautet
könnte was dir ähneln
auch wenn du nie gesungen hast –
oder gegärtnert
schau ich dem Landmann zu
der die Erbsen legt
von fern sind alle Hände
deine
und alle Flüsse tragen dein Boot
und darum sind alle Boote
Kork in meinem Herzen

COMMUNICATION

How intellectually
we talk
while all I want
is to
crawl with you into a hollow tree and

Let's then find a hiding place
in a hollow head

ALL THE BOATS

I go down to the jazz cellars
because of the singer's lips
because of the singer's throat
where there is movement
sound
something might be like you
even if you never sang –
or gardened
I watch the countryman
as he sows the peas
at a distance all hands are
yours
and all the rivers carry your boat
and therefore all the boats are
cork in my heart

SCHLEIFENDE VÖGEL

Es ist alles zu berührt
die Worte
schleifende Vögel, Liebster
ich könnte an Regentagen
für uns Klavier spielen
das Feuer
in den Kamin setzen
ständig seh ich meine Liebe
wachsen sie geht
auf Dächern umher knickt
Straßenschilder nimmt
Autos aus Parkreihen fort
doch du füllst keine Lücke
immer seh ich dich
von irgendeiner Dorfstraße
plötzlich einbiegen
in meine siebenspurige Seele

FLIGHTLESS BIRDS

Everything is tarnished
the words
flightless birds, dearest
I could on rainy days
play the piano for us
light the fire
in the hearth
constantly I watch my love
grow it goes
striding across the roofs bends
street signs removes
parked cars from a row
but you don't fill the gap
I keep seeing you
turning suddenly out of a
village street
into the seven-lane highway of my soul

KÖRNER

ich habe nicht die Fülle der Worte
wie einer der Heu fährt
Heu hat
nur dünn streu ich meine Körner
daß sie die Vögel finden
und Hänsel ihren
Weg

KINDHEIT

Ich hatte den Schlitten
mit den stumpfen Kufen
langsam ging meine Fahrt,
ich stürzte nie und blieb unversehrt.
Während die Sieger im Tal sich ihrer
Wunden rühmten und das Bruchholz
einsammelten, stand ich auf halber Strecke
mit dem Schlitten quer.
Was mir blieb, war ein unauffälliges Schlittern
am Rande der Bahnen.
Nicht ein Schneeball traf mich.
Langsam kroch die Kälte mir
die Knie herauf.

SEED

I don't have an abundance of words
like the haymaker
has hay
I scatter my seed sparingly
so that the birds can find it
and Hansels their
way

CHILDHOOD

I had the toboggan
with unpolished runners
slowly I made my descent,
I never fell off, remained unscathed.
While the victors in the valley boasted
of their injuries and gathered
the pieces of broken wood, I sat halfway
down at right angles.
All I could do was to slither unnoticed
down the edge of the slope.
Not one snowball hit me.
Slowly the coldness crept up
to my knees.

ERINNERUNG

Viola
alte große Geige
Töne wie Zweige streifen mich
das Grün im Herbst wird licht
und meine Spuren füllen sich
mit Kinderträumen schnell
das Instrument das weiße Bettgestell
der große Hof die Augen hell und
überall wächst Heidekraut und
einer ruft spiel nicht so laut

ich meide lang schon diesen Ton
der mir die fernen frohen Tage zeigt
wo einer steht und geigt.

RESTE DES SOMMERS

Wenn herbstlich
die Straßen sich weiten
da die Menschenflut verebbt
geh ich einsamer Sammler
das Strandgut bewahren

Finde die Reste des Sommers
auf den schon windigen Steigen
Nachlaß der heißesten Tage
müder Atem der Stadt

Flacher wird nun das Gefälle
der Wege die wir noch gehen
hin zu verwaisten Ufern
wo still die Boote liegen

MEMORY

Viola
ancient great violin
sounds like willows caressing me
the green in autumn turns to tawny
and my footprints fill up quickly
with childhood dreams of light
the instrument the bedstead white
the spacious yard, eyes shining bright and
all around the heathers crowd and
some one calls don't play so loud

for many years I've shunned that sound
which conjures up those halcyon days
in which a figure stands and plays.

REMNANTS OF SUMMER

In autumn
when the streets grow wider
as the tide of humanity ebbs
I go a solitary gleaner
to beachcomb and preserve

I find the remnants of summer
on the now wind-blown front doorsteps
remainder of the hottest days
weary breath of the town

Less steep becomes the incline
of the paths we still have to go
on to the orphaned river banks
where the boats lie still and low

HAUS IM NORDEN

Leben hier
mit den Wasservögeln
unterm Nebelmond

das stille Dach Himmel
untermauern mit den
Kräften der Seele

säulenhaft
an allen vier Enden

DAS MEER

Dicht bevölkert sind die seichten
Uferstellen dort drängeln wir
im lauwarmen Wasser und treten
einander auf die Füße was
allmählich den täglichen Gruß
ersetzt nur wenige gelangen
über die erste Sandbank in
etwas tiefere Regionen und dürfen
endlich schweigen ganz hinten
wartet das Meer

HOUSE IN THE NORTH

Living here
with the aquatic birds
under the mist-moon

propping up
the still roof of the sky
with the powers of my soul

like pillars
at each of the four ends

THE SEA

Densely populated are the shallows
near the shore where we are jostling
in the lukewarm water and treading
on each other's toes which slowly
takes the place of daily
conversation only a few get
beyond the first sandbank to
somewhat deeper regions and there they can at last
fall silent in the distance
awaits the sea

TERRASSE II

Der Mai hat die zwei blonden
Pferde wieder in die Koppel gestellt
Kokosraspeln
in die Bäume gestreut
eine Handvoll Wespenköniginnen
freigelassen
sie sind völlig friedlich sagst du
als eine auf mich zufliegt
und ich schlage laufe zucke nicht, wie sonst –
laß sie ganz ruhig
an mir suchen und vorbeifliegen
und frage mich
ob ich dir vertraut habe

REGEN

nimm meine Liebe
als einen Regen
der vorüberzieht
du kannst einen Schirm
aufspannen der Wolke
ist es egal

ON THE TERRACE II

The month of May has returned
the two palominos to the paddock
dusted the trees
with dried coconut flakes
released a handful
of Queen wasps
they're quite innocuous you say
as a wasp flies towards me
and I strike out run jump no more, instead –
quite calmly let it
come close examine me and fly on
and ask myself
if I've placed my trust in you

RAIN

please treat my love like
a shower of rain
that will blow over
put an umbrella
up if you want the cloud
won't mind at all

ICH SAH DICH

Du kamst nie
über das Autobahnkreuz
in meiner Schläfe
immer zu Fuß gingst du
ich sah dich schon von weitem
das Gebirg mit den Händen teilen
wie Gebüsch die Meere durchwaten
in eine Wolke schnauben
du warst launig wie ein Bub
ich bedacht wie eine Lehrerin
wir trafen uns am Vormittag
als wärs Unterricht
als wärs lernen fürs Leben.

KLEINE NACHTWACHE

Als letzte gehe ich
ich schließe die Türen zu
und seh mich noch mal um
wenn Euch schon fängt die Ruh

Wenn Euch der Schlaf schon trägt
bin ich noch immer wach
ich geh nochmal vors Haus
und sehe nochmal nach

I SAW YOU

You never came
by the motorway junction
in my temple
you always came on foot
I saw you from afar
dividing the mountains with your hands
wading through seas like they were bushes
breathing fire into a cloud
you as moody as a youth
I as chary as a teacher
we always met in the morning
as if for lessons
as if we were learning for life.

A LITTLE NIGHT WATCH

I am the last to go
I shut doors and windows tight
and have a last look round
when you're all abed at night

When sleep has closed your eyes
I am still wide awake
I go outside once more
another look to take

DIE FISCHER

Die Fischer schlafen.

In ihren Mützen
verlischt
der Meeresschaum

von ihren Augen
fallen die Schuppen
auf die bleichen

Leiber der Fische
die träumen:
die Fischer schlafen.

THE FISHERMEN

The fishermen sleep.

In their sou'westers
sea foam
evaporates

from their eyes
the scales fall
onto the pale

bodies of the fish
who dream that
the fishermen sleep.

BIOGRAPHICAL NOTES

SABINE LANGE was born in June 1953 in Stralsund, in what was then the German Democratic Republic. She grew up in a very musical family and herself won a national prize for music at the age of 13 as the pianist in a piano trio which she formed with two of her brothers. Following her studies in Mathematics and Education, she taught at a secondary school in Feldberg and it was here that she first started to write poetry – as a form of escape, a way of expressing her longing for a different life. She subsequently studied Music and worked as a freelance music teacher and musician until, in 1984, she was appointed archivist in the Hans Fallada Archive in Feldberg. The fifteen years she spent working with the manuscripts and papers of one of Germany's most popular twentieth-century writers proved to be a most productive period in which she began to publish her own poetry as well as essays and books on Fallada. *The Fishermen Sleep*, originally published in German in 1994 as *Immer zu Fuß*, is her first volume of poetry. She has said of her poetry: 'I'm not a political poet – I'm more interested in the landscape of the soul ("Seelenlandschaft")'. The poems in this anthology are mostly poems written in the GDR. The last one in the collection, 'The Fishermen', was awarded the Alfred Gesswein Prize in Austria. Since 1999 Sabine Lange has completed a second volume of poetry and is currently working on the publication of her diaries (1984-1999) as well as a book on the role of the GDR Ministry for State Security ("Stasi") in the formulation of literary policy in the Fallada Archive.

JENNY WILLIAMS is Associate Professor in the School of Applied Language and Intercultural Studies and a member of the Centre for Translation and Textual Studies at Dublin City University, Ireland. She has taught courses in translation theory and practice at undergraduate and postgraduate level, as well as supervised research in the field. Her biography of Hans Fallada, *More Lives than One* (London: Libris, 1998) appeared in German as *Mehr Leben als Eins* (Berlin: Aufbau) in 2002. She is co-author with Andrew Chesterman of *The Map. A Beginner's Guide to Doing Research in Translation Studies* (Manchester: St. Jerome, 2002). This is her first volume of poetry translation.

MARY O'DONNELL is a poet, novelist, translator and critic who is based in Co. Kildare, Ireland. She has published four volumes of poetry, most recently *September Elegies* (2003) and has scripted three series of poetry programmes for the Irish national broadcaster, RTE radio. Her critically-acclaimed third novel, *The Elysium Testament*, appeared in 2004. Her work has been published in literary magazines and journals in Ireland, the UK and the USA and anthologised in collections in Ireland and abroad.

In recognition of her outstanding contribution to the arts in Ireland, she became a member of *Aosdána* in 2001. Membership of this organisation of 200 living Irish artists is by peer nomination and election. In 2005, Mary O'Donnell presented 'Crossing the Lines', a series of radio programmes on European poetry in translation.

Also available in the Arc Publications
'VISIBLE POETS' SERIES
(Series Editor: Jean Boase-Beier)

No. 1
MIKLÓS RADNÓTI (Hungary)
Camp Notebook
TRANSLATED BY FRANCIS JONES
INTRODUCTION BY GEORGE SZIRTES

No. 2
BARTOLO CATTAFI (Italy)
Anthracite
TRANSLATED BY BRIAN COLE
INTRODUCTION BY PETER DALE
(Poetry Book Society Recommended Translation)

No. 3
MICHAEL STRUNGE (Denmark)
A Virgin from a Chilly Decade
TRANSLATED BY BENTE ELSWORTH
INTRODUCTION BY JOHN FLETCHER

No. 4
TADEUSZ RÓŻEWICZ (Poland)
recycling
TRANSLATED BY BARBARA BOGOCZEK (PLEBANEK) & TONY HOWARD
INTRODUCTION BY ADAM CZERNIAWSKI

No. 5
CLAUDE DE BURINE (France)
Words Have Frozen Over
TRANSLATED BY MARTIN SORRELL
INTRODUCTION BY SUSAN WICKS

No. 6
CEVAT ÇAPAN (Turkey)
Where Are You, Susie Petschek?
TRANSLATED BY CEVAT ÇAPAN & MICHAEL HULSE
INTRODUCTION BY A. S. BYATT

No. 7
JEAN CASSOU (France)
33 Sonnets of the Resistance
WITH AN ORIGINAL INTRODUCTION BY LOUIS ARAGON
TRANSLATED BY TIMOTHY ADÈS
INTRODUCTION BY ALISTAIR ELLIOT

No. 8
ARJEN DUINKER (Holland)
The Sublime Song of a Maybe
TRANSLATED BY WILLEM GROENEWEGEN
INTRODUCTION BY JEFFREY WAINWRIGHT

No. 9
MILA HAUGOVÁ (Slovakia)
Scent of the Unseen
TRANSLATED BY JAMES & VIERA SUTHERLAND-SMITH
INTRODUCTION BY FIONA SAMPSON

No. 10
ERNST MEISTER (Germany)
Between Nothing and Nothing
TRANSLATED BY JEAN BOASE-BEIER
INTRODUCTION BY JOHN HARTLEY WILLIAMS

No. 11
YANNIS KONDOS (Greece)
Absurd Athlete
TRANSLATED BY DAVID CONNOLLY
INTRODUCTION BY DAVID CONSTANTINE

No. 12
BEJAN MATUR (Turkey)
In the Temple of a Patient God
TRANSLATED BY RUTH CHRISTIE
INTRODUCTION BY MAUREEN FREELY

No. 13
GABRIEL FERRATER (Catalonia / Spain)
Women and Days
TRANSLATED BY ARTHUR TERRY
INTRODUCTION BY SEAMUS HEANEY

No. 14
INNA LISNIANSKAYA (Russia)
Far from Sodom
Translated by Daniel Weissbort
Introduction by Elaine Feinstein